A
Life Cycle

Nicole Asherah

For the little girl who thought she'd feel sad forever.

Table of Contents

A
Life Cycle

What if you are only ever to be yourself in pieces?
What if "you" is too rich a masterpiece
For someone to view as a whole?
So you are forced to break yourself down
Into digestible pieces,
Like light you secretly contain all
But people can only view what is reflected back to them.

Sometimes I wonder if sunlight gets lonely.

To be seen it has to lose itself in another
So it cannot be without another,
But with another it is never itself.

I often feel like sunlight:
The soft orange glow gliding hesitantly up the sidewalk at dawn,
The harsh midday glare outlining mistakes made,
The sunset fighting against its own retreat.

People never notice the warmth I provide
Until they lose it to the seasons.

Sometimes it's the harmony of chaos
Which quiets the mind,
Chaos flowing into itself like a river bubbles down stones
Smoothing over edges left raw on its own

You bring chaos to me.
But with my own
Harmony rings through our bones.

The world is an orchestra always at play
If you choose to silence your mind
And hear what the musicians have to say

I can offer you peace if you let me.
But it is an active choice you have to make:
Each time,
Every day,
You have to choose to want to exhale.
It is only then I can help your path be unveiled.

I spend more time longing for the past
And dreaming of the future
Than I do experiencing the present.
I let the past stand
As a rating scale to the present
Causing the present
To always fall short
Of warped memories.
What does that say about me?
Or us?
I know I am not alone in this problem.
I was raised to spend my life striving for better
But never learning to be satisfied.
I was taught to cherish the past
Because you'll never be able to relive it.
But what if today was all that mattered?
Wouldn't you spend it differently?

The truth is all we have is today.
And every today we are lucky enough to get thereafter.

You asked me why I craved the city:

Cities of people
Cities of noise
Cities of chaos

Me—a socially anxious introvert who loves nature
Me—someone who finds pleasure in the simplicities of
daily life

You never understood,
I love the struggle.
Not in some artistic melodramatic way,
Don't get me wrong
I wish I could take away all the suffering,
Consume it like a black hole
Crushing it into itself.
But what I love is
Despite the struggle,
The despair,
And the chaos,
Kindness will leak through.

Humanity is most beautiful
When we could choose to be our worst
But decide to be our best.
When there isn't light to be seen,
We make it for others.

You speak words like prayers
Putting faith in the hands of the faithless
And you wonder when your answers will come
But they already came
In the form of all the disappointments
Telling you it's time to turn away

We wait out time,
Wondering if that's what fixes our minds.

Then,

We grow bitter,
Weathered by age
Waiting for time to fix problems
Only people can change

It teetered on the edge of being swept up
Every single time the wind curled under its petals,
But it fought.
It fought
With the only thing that had ever been there for it:
Itself,
The weight it held in the world
Despite its delicate shape
It found roots in its own strength.
So sometimes it shook,
Overwhelmed by the uncontrollable.

But despite the elements,
It never blew away.

A scream rips through the silence,
A battle cry,
For all who have fallen
And all those yet to come.

Oh, arrogant man
Holier than most
You've found purpose preaching to others
To prove you have more to devote.
But there is no truth in your words
Only bravado to cover shame.

In the end,

You will always be to blame
For your pain.
And piety will not forgive you
For all the spirits you tried to claim.

The
Shattering

And the scales tipped just like I knew they would,
Yet I still wasn't prepared for the fall.
But I guess you never do quite fall
When you have a rope to ease yourself down—
No—
You only fall fast
With no ground in sight
You fall
With no relief
No ambulance nearby.
I'm good at falling,
Good at bracing myself for the impact
But pain is pain.
No matter how you prepare
It will always take shape.

And so,
You do what you must,
You heal.

Defeat is inevitable
In the way that Death is
And yet,
They don't necessarily go hand in hand.
Many face Defeat
Before they have ever even contemplated Death—
Not that there really is anything to contemplate
Since Death just is—
Now Defeat,
That's worth contemplating.
Defeat comes for you
More often than anyone cares to admit
And for some it never leaves,
Sparing room only for Death.
Defeat takes something from you
In a way that Death never could,
Defeat takes life.

Life — *the accumulation of love, passion, heartbreak,*
embarrassment, and glee

Some Defeats are small
Only taking a fraction of what you have to give,
While others disarm you
Of everything pumping through your chest
Except blood,
But without everything else,
The blood soon loses its ability to keep you oxygenized.

It's a tragedy.
Yet everyone lays claim to this tragedy
At some point in time.

I think that's what true tragedy is,
The hardships that are inevitable.
Because despite knowing they are to come,
You can never truly brace yourself for their impact.

I don't remember how not to be anxious.

It's as if the weight of the world is always on my shoulders.
I see myself sinking,
Down below water,
I'm out of light's reach.
There are moments of peace
But the minute I try to cling to them
As a life vest,
My hands slip around the edges
And I experience my panic
Just as strongly as the first time.

I know I am failing Them.

But all I can do is cope.

My mind no longer makes sense.
It has always been the sole thing
Keeping me moving forward
But now nothing is sure
And I can't be positive
And I don't want to be negative
So I try not to think at all.
I know I have to press play
But where do I go once in action?
I am not 'Me'
And I am not 'They' either
But if I don't know who 'I' is
How do I fight against 'They' to stay myself?
In a world that constantly hints at me to be something else
I just want an answer.
Because that is what everyone asks of me.
An answer to a question I've never even been sure I know
All I am aware of is the silence that hangs in the air
I think I'm dying,
That's what it feels like.
And I know
It seems like melodramatic words of an angsty artist
But that's what it feels like,
Like I'm 80 years old
Watching Alzheimer's slowly creep through my brain cells
Sometimes there is clarity—
At least clarity of a remnant of the past
But then my eyes glaze over
And I am lost in thoughts I can't explain
I'm probably crazy, melodramatic, and narcissistic.
But since no one will give me the labels I need to seek help
I'll lean into my damaged mentality.

I finally understand why

A Life Cycle

Some people check themselves into psych wards.
I long for that life,
One which follows no societal laws,
It is the closest we get to nirvana
Without putting in the work.

My brain is not safe.

I don't know. I don't know. I don't know. I don't know. I don't know. I don't know. I don't know. I don't know. I don't know. I don't know. I don't know. I don't know. I don't know. I don't know. I don't know. I don't know.

I can't do all of it
So I can't do any of it
I spend my time crying
Slowly dying
I take pity on my privilege
Write myself excuse after excuse
Ignoring my blame
Burying my shame
Then I lean into my hypocrisy
Preaching what I know I can never be

I don't know how to save the world.
I don't even know how to save myself.

I'm left with sorrow,
The broken pieces
Scraping at my open heart.
As I try to offer myself forward
I become a sacrifice to self-declared gods,
And maybe at least my ending will teach
Lessons worth learning
Who is truly deserving?
Is it those who believe they are
And therefore,
Obtain?
Or those who have never seen themselves so
And therefore,
Accept less than?
Or are we all deserving despite our faults?
Despite the greed and insecurity
We sometimes let consume us
Until we are only left with hate.
Or more likely,
It is none of us who deserve the things we desire.
That is why we all spend our lives tipping towards sadness.
Maybe Earth is where gods are sent to atone for sins
Or maybe life is a slot machine
And there is no way to rig what is random
There is only pulling the handle
And facing defeat
Over and over again
Until probability has to grant some form of reprieve—
This reprieve comes in love or kindness or joy—
But only ever lasts long enough
For us to spend it on one moment,
Before we are left with an extra token
To play the odds again
And lose the little security

We managed to win.

It is not the loneliness I fear.
I fear never having my mistakes forgiven
Or my accomplishments commended.
I fear these blurring together
Until all I see are mistakes
Piling up
Pushing me down.
I don't fear being alive
Nor do I fear my thoughts,
I fear that my perception is off
And everyone knows
But no one will come out and say it.
I fear trusting my instincts
Only to have their weight give out under me.
I'm afraid of the fall,
Never the landing.
The fall is the only time I truly lose control
And I'm not really sure what I am without control.
I've never been out of control—not truly.
The closest I've come is in my spurts of anger
But those were shunned more than most of my emotions.
I've learned to allow myself to be angry.
But calm and calculated anger,
Not uncontrollable rage,
Or pain so strong you have to sob it out.
I miss sobbing.
I never really get to do it for the things that matter most.

A Life Cycle

I miss the things that were mine.

I have slowly been losing ownership
Of everything I used to hold dear.
Parts of me
I never knew were capable
Of being ripped from my grasp
Have vanished before my eyes.

It's like a piece of me gets stolen in the night.
And I can deal with individual losses,
I learned to never put all my weight on one leg.
But the sum of no longer having anything
To claim as my own,
It takes a toll.

That toll is me.

Listen to me when I tell you
All I can give is myself.
But myself holds no love,
Not for you,
Not for me,
Truly not for anything.
Love is a currency
I ran out of way before I ever understood its worth.
I've tried to replicate it with kindness and intimacy
But when you hold it up to the light,
It never seems quite right.

My heart hurts
My head aches
It's the only thing that keeps the feelings at bay

My heart is heavy
Sleep didn't provide a long enough reprieve
To free my clogged arteries
So I forfeit today
Under heavy blankets
And dark shades
I try to recreate my resting place.
Oh, let me rest!
From existence
There is stress
I know how to be
Yet the act of being makes me fall apart
At the seams
So let me not
Be
Just for enough time to heal
The inflamed scabs of wounds long past
I know they will settle with time
Yes, time is what I need!
Time to spare
Time not to be
I will take time
Yet I cannot take what is already mine
It is mine to choose
I cannot waste what I'm bound to lose.

I'm vulnerable
In the open
So,
I seek safety
Under warm covers
And false promises,
It's not that I don't crave a life.
It just seems easier
To let it pass me by.

My mind is a hurricane,
Help me find the eye of the storm
I promise one day
I'll be so much more

My weather can do more
Than make others lose form
From me
Roots will sprout.

But until then,
I need you now.

And sometimes light peaks through the clouds
Shifting shadows from my face.
But with time,
The light dims.
Fading into the shadows
Until there is no distinction left.

The
Healing

People say wounds take time to heal.
It's easy to think they're gone
Since it's hard to see their effect sometimes,
But no matter what you do to dress the wounds,
You need time to mend.
I've started to recognize that also applies to life.
We are told we can just fix our problems
And we want to believe that.
There is control in this way of thinking.
Versus recognizing that despite what can be said and done,
Wounds still take time to heal.
But since time is now a commodity,
We worry we won't have enough to fix what is broken
So we don't.
We don't stop.
We keep moving,
Keep injuring ourselves
Until we are falling apart before our very eyes.
We give ourselves enough respite
To put bandages on what needs stitches.
Then, we continue.
With our heads held high
We live,
Racing forwards to the future.

And we wonder why
Blood continues to trail behind us
Wherever we go.

Sometimes losing yourself really means letting go
Of who you used to be.

You are not lost.
You are simply stumbling upon a version of you
You could only see in dreams
And more than anything you are mourning—
Mourning the girl you used to know.
For better or worse,
She's never coming back.
Let yourself grieve the innocence lost
And celebrate the wisdom found.

It is time to become the you that is now.

The thing about healing is
What you are healing from is damage.
You have to claim it.

I say I am damaged.

But that word haunts me in all my moments of intimacy.
It leaks into my instances of anger
And drains my sadness away
Until only despair remains.

I say I am healing.

But it is slow
And I am alone
And nothing makes sense
Yet everything matters
And I'm trying to find identity
But I lose it with every decision I stand for.

So,

I sit,
Letting my senses dull
And sink into hibernation.

Sometimes I wonder if I'm running away…
That once I'm gone
I'll realize
A piece of me missed
What left me broken.
But I think that is just the doubt,
The part of myself I manipulated
Into seeing myself as only flaws

I'm sad to leave it all behind.

Not because it was a life worth living
But because I grew comfortable.
Part of me still fears I won't make it on my own.
What if when push comes to shove
I'm not enough for the life I dreamed of?
Insecurities are fun like that.
They like keeping you trapped in your cycle
But I'm good at surviving the highs and lows that I know
Add in unknowns
And maybe I can't make it anymore,
Maybe I'm not as durable as I like to believe
I concede
I'm scared of pain
I'm afraid that it will lead to the same.
So, which is it?
Do I relish in my rollercoaster of ups and downs?
Or do I fear being stuck on the same ride my entire life?

Every second
Every minute
I am trapped in it
Time
The thing that needs me
The thing that leaves me
You always sound so far away
I live in dreams until the day
Then you go
To be forgotten
Time likes to forget
But never gets lost
I cross my fingers
Praying there won't be a cost
To wasted days
Words I never say
I don't live with regrets
But the shame they never left

A Woman's Bones are of the Earth

A woman's bones are of the earth.
Formed from the forgotten
Lived stories decomposed
Fertilizing a much larger narrative
—a wound.
And our hearts will forever beat in time
With the blood that pours out of it,
It is why we have always been known as healers.
If we did not learn how to tend wounds
We would never have been able to survive
The world we were born into.
But survive we do,
Often even thrive.
Despite the open wound that lives with us
Day to day,

We prosper through the pain.

Empathy lies patiently in the quiet.
It will not push through crowds
Nor demand attention.
It needs the form of a soft caress
From a vulnerable soul
To be accepted into the light of day,
But once accepted
It will plant seeds of hope
Produce plentiful harvests of love and trust,
Even when it wilts,
It only falls to the ground to rebuild.

And maybe empathy doesn't reach light often,
But once it feels its first glimmer of sun
It can never go back.

It is too easy to be filled with noise
Despite our natural inclination favoring silence.
The silence of nature
Not truly silent at all
But harmonious.
Symphonies of symbiosis
Recognizing our need for community.

But we let noise
Fill our heads
Like we let vodka
Fill our stomachs after heartbreak.
Holding no value
Other than to distract,
Yet we let ourselves be taken by such noise
Why?
Because it is common?
Do we ache to conform so much
We will choose suffering simply to fit in?
Sometimes I wonder why...
But more often than not
I don't spare much thought
On people I can't change,

They will find their own way.

I open myself up like a flower
My thoughts
Blossoming petals
I use them to inspire others
To see all the different colors that can be.

But,
Through this reveal,
I leave my center vulnerable
Available for others to feed on
Collecting my nectar as currency
And leaving me bare.

Should I care
That my ideas are still growing?
Just in new soil,

If they have left me,
The source,
To wither away
I say
"Save me before I fade".
Instead they cut me down
Gifting me in celebration
Of those grown
From my decomposition.

I will not let you guide me into self-destructive habits
Shaming my healthy mindset
Till I begin to doubt my ways.
Because I not only know my worth,
I know yours,
And it is worth more than you give.

So,
Trap yourself
In your destructive habits—
If you must.
But you will never be able to lock me away again.

One foot in front of the other
I keep moving
Forward
Away from all I left behind

One foot in front of the other
I only look back to remember forgotten scars
But I don't linger long enough to lay them to rest

One foot in front of the other
I don't stop
I can't stop
If I do
I'll collapse
Under the weight
Of all the feelings I've yet to escape

One foot in front of the other
I look forward to a life I long to meet
But with every step forward
It seems longer until we greet.

Sometimes the heaviness is there
To keep you from floating a w a y . . .

Please handle me with care,
I'm sensitive to others' indentations
Becoming mine.
I'm sick of becoming something I'm not
Eroded by the pressure of those who handle me
Just hold me,
Cradle my sensitive spots
Like a newborn's head
I need support.
The weight of my mind is too much
For my body to bare most days.
I spend more time upside down
Than I'd like to admit
It doesn't keep me from functioning
Just distorts my perspective,
Preventing me from trusting
What is right before my eyes
Because I fear being swept up in lies.

Stuck in a constant state of vulnerability,
I am delicate skin
Easy to rip open.
Too many people have left me bleeding out
And I'm running low on thread
To stitch myself up again

I don't know when I became something
Other than what I used to be.
It didn't happen all at once,
But I never really noticed a shift
Until I woke up one day
To a new person looking back at me.

People want a piece of something I no longer have to give.

I consistently fall victim
To a cycle of giving myself too freely.
I yearn for everyone to have what I lack.
But you cannot give to people
What they don't want to take.

More Than a Moment

My hardships need to be numbered
Kept in a box
Contained to be digested and dissected
Because it needs to make sense.

I need to make sense.

Understand
That my pain is not understandable
Just like my joy
They are chemicals in my brain
That even science can't explain.

You want answers I just can't give
A way to frame my pain
When simply put
No pain is the same.

I pride myself on my clear perception
And yet often times my vision
Ends up being the most clouded.
Both from fantasies and insecurities
I spin around in my head
Until I am sick.
Then I shut down to repair
Before I wake
Only to repeat the cycle
I continue to create.

Oh, little girl,
Labelled naïve
They saw fault in your belief
Because theirs' had died
With their dreams

Oh, little girl,
How they laughed
And how you cried
And how they grew angry
And how you apologized

Oh, little girl,
Screaming out
You asked for help
But they never failed
To let you down

Oh, little girl,
You blamed yourself
For lacking a home
Learned to find safety in sadness
And called it your own

Oh, little girl,
How you got lost every time they left
You stumbled down dark roads
But you never needed guidance to find your way back
To the seeds you were meant to sow

Oh, little girl,
You ran away
But nobody followed
To see if you were okay

They claimed they never knew what to say

Oh, little girl,
You were always enough
Their confidence was simply a bluff
To hide the fear from how brightly you shined
With you they were afraid they'd have to come alive

And oh, little girl,
I'm sorry I couldn't save you.

But oh, little girl,
How you will grow
Big and tall
Above it all

You will exercise your strength
And save yourself from their mistakes

She used to pick flowers
Wrapping fingers around stem
With intention,
Pulling up from root
Claiming a singularity.
Before scouring for the next
Life worthy of her gaze.
Her calculations only ended
When she was satisfied
With how the colors melted into meaning.

Then,
She ran.
With uncontained joy
With panting breath
With wide smiles and sweaty hands
She presented her bouquet,
Hoping her message of love would translate.

Forced smiles were gifted
Before pleasantry faded
Their backs faced her once more
As they became busy with before
An impenetrable wall
Even love couldn't get to fall.

She walked away
With heavy steps,
Until,
She saw another face
She believed a smile deserved a place.

I remember tiptoeing down halls
And grazing seats
Rarely walking on grass
And always checking my back
I remember softly treading upstairs
And sneaking through back rooms
Staying where the TV could light up the gloom.
Living in the glow of its fantasies
It was the closest thing to love
I was allowed to see.

I remember turning knobs slowly
And peaking in
I remember holding my breath
To see what mood they were in
I remember counting down days
And growing up fast

I remember no longer living there
Is when I got my life back.

And when I didn't like anything,
I liked the car.
It meant change,
Going to and from
The in-between
It was a goodbye and a hello
There was never a choice in which way to go

An Idea of a Daughter

How am I supposed to feel
When I see the shame
She carries in my name?
And yet,
She doesn't see it
As a reflection of her feelings towards me.
She likes my heart
Because it reminds her of a time
When she was able to hold warmth.
But she tells me to cover up and hide
Because she claims others can't handle my shine.
Really it is her who is blinded by the glare.
She often forgets I'm there.
Underneath the bluster,
And that my flames can be stamped out
But only by those who dare to get close
Yet no one ever truly does,
Except for her.

One day
I would like her to be proud of me
Not just the person she edited me to be.
Edit my imperfections
And lose me in the process.
My imperfections and quirks are beautiful.
They are what turn me into a person,
Not just an idea of one.
I know living as an idea is what keeps her holding on
But it has always been the beginning of my unraveling.

Please let me be a person.

We are alive in only this time
To make mistakes
To make discoveries
To make stories

Let me make mine.

What hurt the most is that you knew I was scared.
You knew my insecurities laid close to my heart
And you wanted me to let you near
Enough to touch the scars,
To comfort my fears away you said.
But instead
You piled them on top of me.

I had just started to get distance between myself and them
But now I feel consumed again
Lost in a haze of doubt
Unable to find clarity
My head spins with every good and bad thing
Trying to make sense
Trying to find truth
But I am lost
With no one to turn to.

Because I made the mistake of believing
You could finally think of me,
Instead of leading with your own insecurities.

I don't need you to love me.
I need you to accept me,
To see me as a person
Separate from your wants & whims.

What do you want me to say?
I try to explain
But you live in the lies
Tangled in webs of your own design
I find myself giving up every time.

Should I record all we ever say?
So years from now I have proof
When you try to use fiction against me?

You say you want me to feel
You say you're glad that I healed
But somehow none of your words feel real.

When will it be about me?
I shouldn't need to scream to be seen
When will you see it is you,
The cause of the pain
I went through.

But your words are only right
When they come straight from my mind

Why will I never feel your love
Never believe I am good enough
Is it you
Is it me
Or is it just our history?

As a little girl,
I was encouraged just enough to see the dreams
But not enough to believe they could be for me,
And isn't that kind of worse?
Dangling the possibilities just out of reach
Only being a cheerleader for others to succeed

Sometimes
I believe I am more than I am.
Sometimes
They believe I am more than I am.
But the truth is,

I shall always fall short of less than I am capable of.

I'm learning to make mistakes.
I was never taught it was a part of life
I grew up learning it was a crisis,
Something you can never take back
Always on your record
To decide whether you're good or bad.

Despite more of my life
Being filled with a fire
To survive
I tend to want to die
After the smallest of goodbyes

I want to be the sun.
Sometimes I'm able to catch a flame
But I quickly turn to ash,
Like a used match
I crumble under my own weight

A Life Cycle

I have a habit of not truly saying what I mean
But in that people find beauty

Do you feel alone
As you stare up at the sky
Full of meaning
But always lost to the eyes,
It makes me think of life.
And how sad I am,
To finally be alive
Overwhelmed by feelings
I'm not even sure are mine
I let them flow through me
At least it passes the time.

Does anyone ever find what they're looking for?
Are we all destined to feel alone?
Sometimes,
I lose hope.

I often dream of slowing down raindrops
I long to follow their path
Past the splash
To recognize each individual stride
Before seeing the collage that is a storm
I wish to observe the act of dying and being reborn.

Do you feel alone
As you stare at the stars in the sky
Knowing no one can see
How brightly you shine
Or is that just me?
It's why I ask you to speak.
Envelop me in your endless needs
Your words give me space to breathe.

A Life Cycle

We always seem to fall separately
Despite being built up together.
We lose each other
When the heaviness becomes too much,
It is only gravity that keeps us company then.

The fall is swift
But it can feel like flying
Holding your breath
Right before hitting the earth
It's never soft
Always a collision
With a force opposite to our own make up
Breath knocked out
And an environment unknown,
There is infinity in that moment.

But at some point,

Past infinity,

We come together with those we lost along the way.

If I asked you to sit with me,
Would you know what I mean?
Because I can't keep explaining to you
How to love me.
At some point
You just have to know.

I've got to remember to let the light in,
Moments in my head
Feel like days lived over again
I get relief in sleep
But then I dream,
It's all nightmares in the end.

Light

Shines

Through

It is not everyone's path
But I don't walk this road alone

Riddled with scars
I see who you are
The strength in your healing
The power in your feeling.

I will never truly know
How far you fell
How dark it got
How close we were to never meeting

But you found strength
To keep your heart beating,
In your happiness,
I've learned meaning.

I've broken into the mess you see
I've broken into every piece I've longed to be
I've broken into my version of a masterpiece

So cry,

Let your eyes flood
With all the wrongdoings you've ever faced
Or forced someone else to take.

Cry because it hurts
Cry because it doesn't
Cry because it's over
Cry because you're healed
Cry because you're happy
Cry because you don't even know how it happened

Just cry,
Because it means something.
And meaning something matters.

You know what they don't tell you about living?
When you truly are,
You can't be contained.
You are an explosion of renewable fuel
Nothing can truly keep you.
There is beauty in that,
Sometimes even peace in the chaos
But once you realize nothing can keep you,
You start to realize that also means no one can keep you.
People can admire your flame,
Help temper pieces,
Even fuel your light's expansion,
But no one can truly hold your ever-exploding pieces.
They become collateral damage in your expansion.

So, living comes at a cost,

But the only other option
Is to stamp out your flame for others to feel okay.

Soften your edges
Smoothing over the hard definition
You've had to maintain to remain intact
Once a cherished monument
Now a rigid tomb
Limiting your expansion.
Let cracks show
Add pressure
And seep through them
Test your fragile insides on fresh air
But don't lose your shape completely,
It's okay to seek refuge in your walls
When the outside world offers harm,
But you are not living in a constant war zone anymore.
There is no need to leave your walls shut
When only allies lay at the door,

Welcome them.

The willing
You have waited all this time for
Extend your arm in offering
Feel your hand clasp theirs'
Melt into the warmth of trust,

You are safe.

We lose a lot to history.
More often than not we lose love,
We trade it in for self-serving motivations
And yet,
All we seem to strive for in the present day is love:

Love of lovers
Love of achievement
Love of peers
Love of duty

We act as if love is a modern-day currency
As if it didn't finance the motivation
Of the people who walked the earth before us.
Historians will turn stories of love and loss
Into stories of greed and glory
With claims of marriage only for safety,
They demote the depth of feeling experienced
By those no longer living.
I don't argue against the purpose of these marriages
Nor do I interject
Husbands and wives found love of lovers
In each other with time
But I do argue that the same loves existed,
Guiding farmers to fight in wars
And eldest siblings to marry those of a higher status.

"Who cares? These people are long forgotten now."
But one day we will be them,
No longer able to add truth
To the narrative constructed around us.

I've never been someone who cares to be remembered,
Probably because I know my narrative drained of love

Creates a narrative that is no longer me
So, either way,
I am forgotten.
Just like history always is.
I think that's why
We have never truly been able to learn from our past.
Because all we are really told are stories,
Fables we craft
To fit what we believe is proof of our betterment
Not realizing these stories keep us trapped
In a cycle of our own disillusionment.

I've always believed we make choices in life:

Choices to be kind
Choices to do the right thing
Choices to be happy

Life may happen to us
But we decide how we respond

I have confidence
In the fact that I don't know
But those who believe they know
Only know nothing,
Knowing nothing is only similar
To knowing something
By the way they both can lead to mistakes.
But with one,
You have the ability to learn something new.

The truth is everyone is dancing to their own melody.
Even if this song is altered
To align itself with a genre of preference
Everyone lets their authenticity slip
Through the Auto-Tune
And then feels the burden of regret
As their song seems to lose the ability
To be a calculated hit.

But genres are always changing,
And if all you do is simply match the tones
Of everything that has already been sung,

You will find yourself lost in empty sounds.

I want to live in the quiet
The soft sounds of nature
Fueling me to find myself
The quiet
Where there is space to be
Without judgement
We let ourselves go
Sinking into biology
I exist in the quiet
That is what no one is yet to see
It is not me in the noise
Just a body

Sometimes I think I was meant to be born water.
I was meant to hold no shape
And be fluid in my ways,
The only thing that ever seems to bring
A semblance of peace to my spirit
Is when I am in water,
Being near
At least quenches the thirst of freedom
In fantasy.
I was meant to be fluid
Lingering through life in waves
Leaving ripples in my wake
Soft in sound
Yet,
Roaring
In purpose
Sent down from the heavens
To show the nature of existence
In its rawest form
I am water.

Sunlight

You run orange over my skin
Skating light down my dips
Tickling the blood within,
You are the warmth of touch from a familiar lover
Confident in your placement on me,
You creep down my spine
Telling my life in time
And my time in life.
You are a lifeline to shifting tides
So, I align my life with yours.

Without you,
I am always wanting more.

I have always been a butterfly
Living a life of cycles,
Each new me is an epiphany.
But I will forever cherish my past molds,
I carry their pieces inside of me
My wings a shifting mosaic of the life I led.

It's the sun caressing my skin
The sweet smell of the trees
That makes me see life as it is.
We all crave sin
Yet rarely appreciate the earth
As it falls on our lips
But I breathe it in
Relish in a realm of energy
Flowing free like the atoms born in the beginning
Living is not simply existing.
I've tried to crave societal delights
But found influence to be empty
Money to be weighted
And beauty to only be found in creation.
I will leave these treasures for you
To leave or abuse
I'm addicted to a much purer perfume.

I would like to be without me
To finally be free
In the wind
My thoughts flow
From my mind
No longer weighed down
By my body
I would be a force of nature
Summoning myself from the elements
Discarding all the pollutants
That have tried to taint my system

A Life Cycle

It's the little things that affect you the most:

A special greeting
A welcomed hug
A ray of sunshine

It is so easy to let your mind encase you
In a tomb of your own misery
Like Indiana Jones
There are trials and tribulations
That make you rethink your effort
But once the light cracks through your tomb
You are able to see the gleam of the treasure
That is you

I've never liked possibilities.

In my world,
Unpredictability always ended
Worse than could be imagined.
I think that's why I struggle to love life.
Because the only difference
Between life and death
Are possibilities.
I've always felt safer in death
There is no option of it hurting
More than it already does.
Because in life
When every cell of my body is in agony
And I can't see the pain getting worse
It can,
It always can.
Just like it can always get better,

I often forget happiness has no peak.

I worry too much
About what people will think
Of the fact that I care,
Why can I not love freely?
I shame my passion away
Until I am nothing
But a hollow shell of a person,
Then I feel sorry for myself
For not loving
For barely living
Yet,
It is I alone
Who asks myself
To feel less than I deserve.

I have so much love to give.
My heart always seems to be heavy
Weighed down by every person's individual pain
I long to take in,
All the heartbreak.
But in pain
We learn to find love
And in love
We find joy
And with joy
We make beauty.
The beauty of life
Is that it's not designed to make you feel happy.
Remember how people always say it's the journey,
Not the destination,
We learn to enjoy things
Because of the struggle it took to get there.
It's beautiful and it's tragic
And it's the only thing we have.

It's life.

I teem with thoughts and emotions
Feeling guilt
For both their expression and non-expression
Resort to turning off my mind instead
I simply do not know how to contain my feelings.

I believe I tend to catastrophize things
Exploding them or ignoring them
Lacking a channel to maintain balance
I lean into annoyance and indifference
To help taint their extremities

I would like to learn how to let myself break
I try too hard to pick up the pieces
Before they have ever even taken shape
It just prolongs my destruction
Making me claim it as part of my own
I hold the breaking too close to my soul

I let the feeling flow through me,
Filtering out all the love and hate
I hold too close
An exorcist of souls not mine
I am cleansed.

In my empty vessel
There is hope to begin again.

If I could fly
Where would I go
I'd like to have a place
To call home
Somewhere to land
Let my feet sink in
Make roots,
Grow…

I've never needed clear skies
To find beauty outside
I've never needed a planned life
To know it's not mine

With the sun warming my skin
You're the closest to love I've ever been
It melts away my callous heart
Please know it wasn't mine from the start

And after breaking,
The light bleeds through my pieces:

Light so pure all thoughts are cleansed
Leaving an ecstasy
No drug has ever granted me.
I would long to plant a soft kiss on every forehead
If I could transfer this euphoria in a caress,

I hope my words will do instead.

The
Loving

The first thing I noticed about her was her energy.
She seemed to radiate excitement
For even the ordinary.

She said I made her nervous
And I held my breath
As she kissed me goodbye.
She guided me through the crowded room
An anchor to my mind.

When endless chatter numbed the air,
We exchanged coy smiles
And leaned in close,
Whispering words
We had never thought before.
I told her
She deserved more
Than she gave herself.
We laughed through kisses.

Lying in her arms,
The weight of my world didn't feel as heavy.

God how your eyes shined
With our heads only inches apart
As we laid side by side on your bed.
I never wanted that moment to end,
Not even with a kiss,
I just wanted to see you.
I wanted to memorize every inch of your face,
The way your lips moved
Over each sound of every word you spoke.
I barely remember what we spoke about.
All I remember was you asked me questions
No one ever cared to ask before—
Not deep cliché ones—
No,
Instead you asked me to describe my old place in London
Because I told you it was my dream room.
No one had ever held such curiosity
For the small ponderings in my head.
I wish I caressed your face
To give you a moment
To bask in my adoration.
You were good at that—
Admiring me.
But I was too shy,
Too new to these feelings
And too afraid of being vulnerable
To use the right words
To make sure you knew how lucky I felt.
For that I am sorry.
I hope you felt it in the way I chose you
Because I don't choose people often—
Almost never—
And you knew that.
You could tell I rarely let people into my intricacies.

I didn't even mean to let you in
And yet somehow you eased my walls down,
Enough to leave the memory of you
Lingering within me.

You kissed my lips
And I had to pause for breath
I simply couldn't believe something so pure
Could exist outside my head

I'm falling out of the feeling,
I never truly believed I'd get to feel it in the first place
So I know I should be grateful
I mean—
I am grateful.
But the come down from the extraordinary
To the ordinary is more chilling than I ever imagined.
I always wanted to believe
I'd be mature enough to just feel grateful
For my glimpse at something only seen in stories,
And yet,
That feeling was as addictive as any drug,
It changes you.
It brings back a you
You never thought existed.
I don't even know if it's her I want,
Or just the feelings she brought out in me.

Love me like I am whole
And I will love you like you're here

I fabricate worlds
Where we are happy again
Your kisses a lifeline
For you,
I'll wait a whole lifetime.

What if you were it for me
Too good to be
Not truthfully
If only I could see
We loved in fantasy

You never really let yourself be seen
I think that's how you liked it,
Being a daydream

I'm going to say it,
I want someone to love me.
I want to be adored.
I want their hands to never get enough of me
Because they just can't believe
Someone like me exists in the flesh.
I want them to double text me
And triple text me
Because they know
Their thoughts are always welcome in my head.
I want to catch them gazing at me
At the most random of times
And make a blush blossom on their cheeks
As I tease them about their staring.
I want them to shower me with kisses
Just so I never forget
How loved I am.
I want them to notice
When my mood shifts
And let me talk about it with open ears
Or cuddle it away.
I want them to annoy me
With their favorite movies
And songs
And jokes
And them.
I want them.
And I want them to just want me.

I seem to be making up for lost time
In the category of feelings.
I spent years forcing myself not to care
And not to crave
And now that I am teaching myself
How to lean in to life,
I teem with a tidal wave of feelings
At the simplest of gestures
Desperately seeking admiration
Since my first taste.

I don't want to be that type of person,
I don't want to need people to love me.

And we are all schoolgirls again
At the first sign of affection,
Or at least I am.

My love hurts most days,
I'm at the stage
Where I can see the possibility of it
Being taken away
Any day now,
It's strange
How your heart can break
For something that hasn't happened yet.

I don't regret the act of loving
But I do admit
Sometimes the pain is too harsh
To be met,
I seek distance from my love.
It's the act of closing our eyes
We humans love to do.
Closing our eyes to tragedy
An act of selfishness,
Where we often close more than our eyes
We close our minds.
We pretend these tragedies aren't daily
I don't blame humankind,
Because it's truly the only way to survive.

I miss the way you talked
Like you had no fear of the world,
You talked like it was yours to conquer.
For a second,
I wasn't as scared of living
With you by my side.

I want to be your one and only
Not just a way
To make the days less lonely

I miss the way it used to be.
I miss the ease with which I would wrap around you,
Finding comfort in your heat.
It was second nature.
Our bodies fitting together
In a jumbled pile of limbs,
Squeezed together in places not meant to be
—and yet were.
We unconsciously leaned into each other;
Into intimacy,
Into trust.
But now—
Now there is a wall between us at the best of times.
Sometimes we try to pretend.
You fall into my arms
And I hold tight
But our limbs fumble,
Elbowing each other
Like people searching for candles in a blackout.
When we do finally settle,
I grow suffocated by your weight
And you by my heat.
We no longer know each other's edges.

With you
Life was a movie,
But we were nothing
Once the credits ended.

I can show you what life can truly be
If only you let me.
We could be free
In a land of sun rays and laughter.
There may be dirt on our feet
But oh, the earth feels so sweet,
Like the gentle touch of a long-lost lover
—it welcomes you back.
As if you didn't spend years
Running away from its life.
It loves you in that forever kind of way.
Souls see souls
When they come out to stay.
So,
Stay,
Bare and vulnerable with me,
Feel the elements break us down
And build us back up again.
Life is a cycle
But it doesn't have to be of pain.
Life is a cycle of growth and regrowth
Like perennials
We bloom more than once.

I love you because you try
And you try because I love you

You love me because I try
And I try because you love me

i love you softly
When you fall asleep in my arms
While I'm telling you a story
I LOVE YOU LOUDLY
When you keep making dumb jokes
Until I snort with laughter
I love you bravely
When you tell me your fears of the future
I love you fearfully
When I tell you my dreams for the future
I love you a little
When you make fun of my sneezes
I love you a lot
When you randomly bring me food at work
But the one thing I never do,

Is love you less.

The hardest thing someone can do is love another person.
It is why you shouldn't love easily.
Yes, send love to all who come your way
But do not love them,
Because loving takes pieces of you.
It is only worth it
If you are given their pieces in exchange
So you both are whole
In a completely new way.

Q & A

What inspired A Life Cycle?

A Life Cycle was inspired by one of the darkest years of my
life. I never planned on writing a book while I was writing
it. I simply was writing poetry in my journal throughout the
year like I always do. The book begins in February 2019
when I started backpacking around South East Asia. After
about a month and a half of traveling, I arrived in Lombok,
Indonesia, for a volunteer home stay helping children learn
English. On my second day, I was sexually assaulted by the
local man I was staying with who had created this program.
My sexual assault brought all these wounds from childhood
to the surface in more vivid detail than ever before. The 4
sections of A Life Cycle follow the year of my life after my
sexual assault. I didn't know who I was or what I wanted
most of time but by writing these poems, going to therapy,
and releasing old trauma, I became a person I never
imagined I could be. I became a person I am so incredibly
proud of. The truth is I felt so alone during this process of
transformation which is why I decided to publish A Life
Cycle. There have been many books in my life that have
given me the words I needed just when I needed them but
there was nothing for me during this dark period of
transformation. I know that my words can now offer
something I lacked for others who are experiencing any
kind of emotional turmoil and deep change.

Why did you split A Life Cycle into sections?

A Life Cycle was split into sections to emphasize the
process of growth. But when you look into each section

you will find dark feelings on the lighter sections and hopeful feelings in some of the darkest sections. I did this with the intent to show that healing isn't linear. After great joy we can still fall into dark thoughts. This doesn't mean you are going backwards. It just shows you found another layer in need of healing to become an even better version of yourself.

Why doesn't the story begin with The Shattering?

The story doesn't begin with The Shattering because no one's story begins with their breaking. I believe it is important to show we are never this whole other person with no underlying problems. Yes, there is often an event that pushes us over the edge to reach our darkest corners. But these corners still existed from all the small hurts we faced throughout our life. It feels dismissive of one's own strength, pain, and identity by not showcasing who one is before the shattering.

What is the two-poem break in the beginning section before The Shattering?

The two-poem break in A Life Cycle is supposed to capture the traumatic moment one experiences that tips you over the edge. I started writing "Oh arrogant man" 10 mins before I was sexually assaulted. While that poem displays my specific traumatic event, I hope it also stands as a representation for all. It showcases the hurt and betrayal one feels from trauma because you constantly question what you did to deserve it. In reality, it is often another's ego that is at fault.

Why do most of the poems not have titles?

I am not the biggest fan of adding titles to my poems. I only add them after the poem has been written if they add meaning to the poem as whole. But most of the time, I already feel like the poem is complete. I could simply choose a title that summarizes the poem or a key line from it, but I've found it subtracts from the meaning.

Why did you title the book A Life Cycle?

The title A Life Cycle came to me very quickly once I started editing the book. I read it almost a year after writing it for editing purposes. Despite remembering the exact scenarios that inspired these words, I felt like I connected to the words in a totally new way. We mistakenly think of a life cycle as something only experienced once. We are born, we grow up, we grow older, and then we die. But I see humans as "perennials, we bloom more than once". We are constantly becoming new versions of ourselves but the only way to become a new version of yourself, is to leave behind an old version. This book is a guide for those moments of change, pain, and discovery.

What is the meaning behind the cover?

Because I am a visual artist, as well as, a writer, the look of my book was very important to me. I chose to have an Azalea bush going through the stages of its life cycle on the cover because it seemed like a good representation of the meaning behind the title. I chose an Azalea bush in particular because it is believed to symbolize self-care, remembering your home, passion that is still developing and fragile, and abundance. I see it as once you go through this cycle of self-care, you find the home within yourself. This allows you to discover your passions and abundance. I chose a pink version of the flower because pink often stands for self-love and youthfulness. I truly believe the only way to heal and grow as a person is to reconnect with your inner child which is why I find the representation of youthfulness invaluable. I went with a light purple as the background cover to bring the reader a sense of peace whenever they grab their copy.

Acknowledgements

First off, I would like to thank everyone who took the time to read my book. I am eternally grateful to each and every one of you. I may have written this book, but it belongs just as much to you guys as it does to me now.

I could never have imagined what a feat publishing this book would be which is why I have such immense gratitude for the people in my life that supported me through the process. My most heartfelt thank you goes out to my mom. She has always been the biggest supporter of my writing even when she became the subject of certain pieces. She was there for me throughout every step of creating this book. I truly would have been completely unhinged without her constantly being available to let me vent, think out loud, and ask questions she didn't have answers for.

I have deep gratitude for Joel Ronkin, my high school creative writing teacher. He was instrumental in helping me develop confidence in my writing while showing areas my work could grow and develop. Despite leaving high school long ago, he is the most meaningful teacher I have ever had. Thank you for helping edit my book and encouraging my success all these years.

I would like to thank Brian Fienblum, my publicist, for guiding me through the business aspects of this book and giving me the space to create the path I dreamed of for my book. I am so grateful to my dear friend, Amanda Shanely, for editing my book, inspiring my creativity, and encouraging me throughout the process. I would also like to thank my friend, Lulu Octeau, for advising and editing A Lifecycle.

I have an immense amount of gratitude for my therapist Wendy for helping me heal from my traumas. She was my support system while I was writing this book and then encouraged me throughout the process of bringing this book to life. I'm also really grateful to my brother for always helping me with technical problems and giving advice on how to achieve my goals. In addition, I would like to thank Vaibhav Tyagi for designing the book art I spent months dreaming up.

Lastly, I would like to thank everyone who has encouraged my writing and supported my dreams. Every kind word continues to sit with me and fill my heart with love.

Nicole Asherah

Nicole Asherah is an artist based in Los Angeles, CA whose main mediums are poetry, film photography, and abstract oil painting but she has a habit of dabbling in whatever sparks her creative juices. Switching between mediums of expression, Nicole tries to connect readers to intimate moments, feelings, and relationships experienced throughout life.

Nicole has the unique background of being raised by a psychologist, backpacking around more than 15 countries by herself, attending Roehampton University's Creative Writing Poetry MFA, volunteering with SURJ and other grassroots organizations that have all synthesized to give her a broad understanding of people's individual struggles and how to capture them in art.

Find more of Nicole Asherah's work at nicoleasherah.com

9 798985 187106